The Infinite Destiny

- - words and block-prints by Gwen Frostic

reen majesty –

the nexus of all life . . . .

The millions of leaves upon each tree =
every blade of grass that grows = =
the mosses = lichens = = ferns
and all the flowers on earth =
each bit of green = =
ceaselessly transmutes
air = water = = and
the energy of the sun
into living food . . . .

Green majesty –
without which there
could be no other life . . .

Green majesty – –
the ancient and everlasting promise
of an infinite destiny . . . .

s the dense mists =

the steam clouds that enveloped the planet earth

began to disperse =

solar energy was developing

a very simple organism . . . . . .

From that tiny speck of life =

through billions of ages

and multitudinous changes =

through the rise and fall of endless forms

the green world emerged . . .

And ever after wherever green plants grew

animals and humans followed . . .

Animals lived and became extinct =

empires were built and lost = =

their fate resting upon the green world of nature . . . .

A plant – –

life from air and water – an alluring process –
each a distinct individual – able to carry on
all the essential needs of its own life –
while striving to grow unto itself . . . .

Slowly plants advance and retreat in response to
climate – migrating to areas most favorable to
their particular needs . . . .

Each green life bears the insignia of its kind –
while growing without limits – indefinite in pattern
– carrying youth forever at its tips –
growing stronger with age –
the very essence of freedom within its realm . .

Its branches may reach in endless directions –
forever regenerating themselves –
its leaves may be large or small –
stems tall or short
the color of its flowers may differ widely
from others in its family –

as the winds = the sun = =
the soil and the water
influence its being . . . . .

Its only objective is to grow . . . .

It is during the miracle of springtime
that the green world seems most intimate = =
when the tips of all the trees glow with new
growth = bringing assurance of perpetual youth .

Each plant grows through its ability to adjust =
= unrestricted by specialization =
free to follow innumerable alternatives
as conditions shift . . . .

The pace of change expedites
the alacrity of development . . .

And so = = as the earth circles the sun
in unchanging rhythm =
bringing season after season
each with its own beauty and purpose = =
life = = in its own time and place
will be as eternal as the grasses . . . . . .

o deny the future

is to deny the wondrous capabilities of nature –

its infinite sources of strength and energy = = =

the multitudinous ways it incessantly

creates alternatives . . . . .

Ecological variations = =

the tributaries of evolution =

and cosmic time create a manifold of options

attuned to all potentialities . . . .

Nature = = ever perpetuating itself = = =

is exhaustible only to the mind

that has lost the sense of wonder . . .

It demands deep inspiration = =

immense knowledge and understanding

for the human mind to perceive

that in the seeds of the present

lie a radiant tomorrow = =

– and go on = =

forever searching = =

= forever believing . . . . .

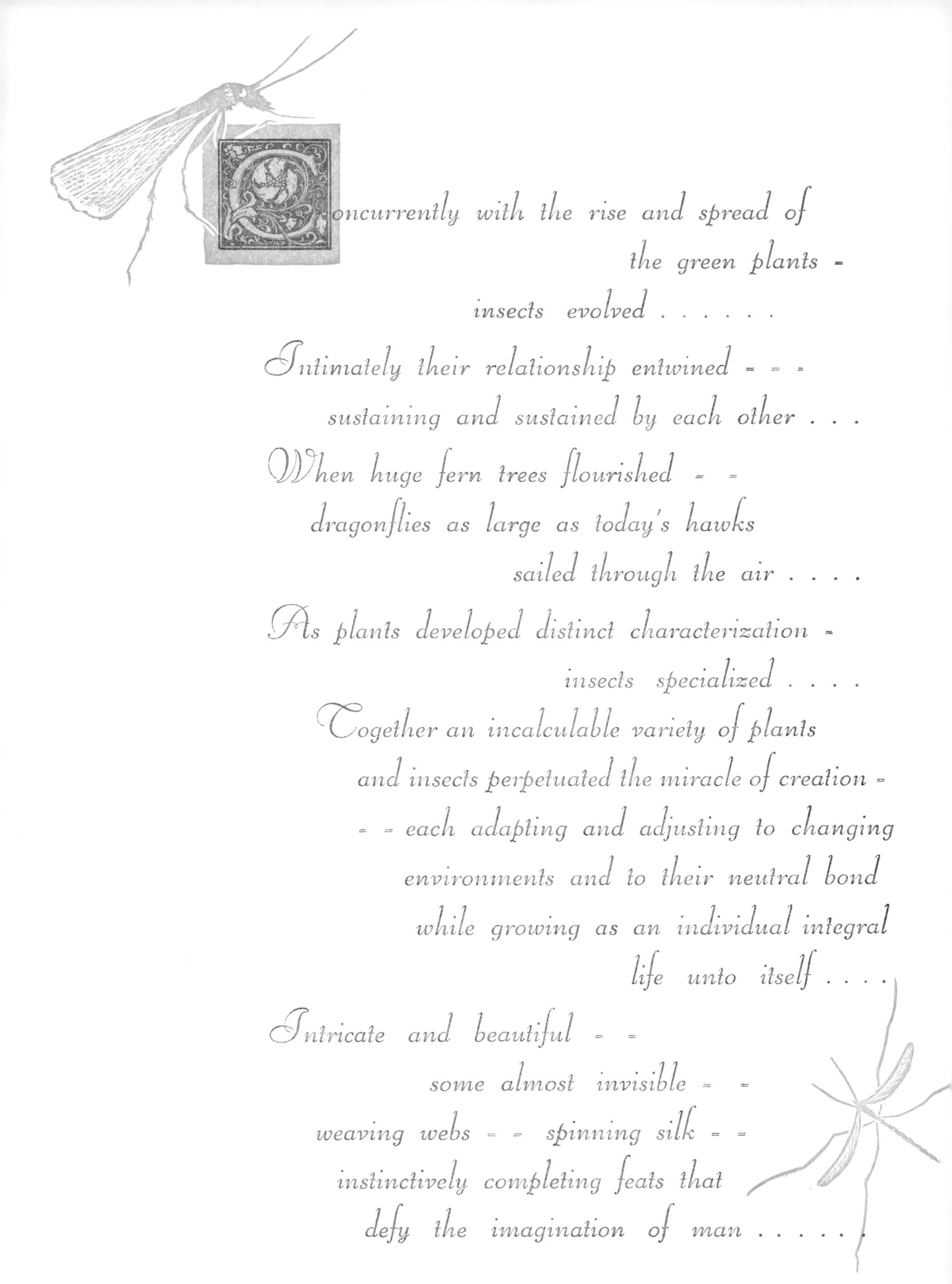

Concurrently with the rise and spread of
the green plants -
insects evolved . . . . . .
Intimately their relationship entwined - - -
sustaining and sustained by each other . . .
When huge fern trees flourished - -
dragonflies as large as today's hawks
sailed through the air . . . .
As plants developed distinct characterization -
insects specialized . . . .
Together an incalculable variety of plants
and insects perpetuated the miracle of creation -
- - each adapting and adjusting to changing
environments and to their neutral bond
while growing as an individual integral
life unto itself . . . .
Intricate and beautiful - -
some almost invisible - -
weaving webs - - spinning silk - -
instinctively completing feats that
defy the imagination of man . . . . .

Industrious = = and efficient = = =
gleaming jewels of the air
with infinite ways of meeting
the challenge of survival . . . . . .

Born from eggs = =
omnifarious in colors =
sizes = = shapes = and adornments - -
deposited with great ingenuity
to meet the vicissitudes of weather
and evade the many lives searching
for them . . . .

From these eggs a tiny life comes forth =
= = to eat = = = which seems to be its sole
reason for being . . . .

Long before the age of man =
tiny caterpillars defoliated trees =
as they do even unto this day = =
= and always the trees continue to grow
without the help of man ! !

A mystery man cannot comprehend . . . .

Having one of the shortest life spans
of all earth's living creatures –
these many segmented organisms shed their
skins many times before they spin a cocoon
of substance produced by their own bodies -
in time winged adults emerge - - -
leaving behind an intricate cast
from which a life has flown . . . .

The miracle of transformation
unique to insect life . . . . .

A life marvelously contrived –
with alacrity of motion - -
- - jumping - swimming -
running - - flying

With excellent vision and hearing
and sensory ability to detect the faintest
odor and the slightest vibrations . . . .

Each using to the fullest
the sense upon which its life depends . . . . .

It needs no other . . . . !

Theirs was one of the first live sounds
to break the primeval stillness = =
making sounds without voices = =
communication by touch = scent =
tapping and scratching = =
= the essence of simplicity . . . .
Life is hazardous = =
encountering drought = heat = cold = storms
and millions of lives intent on
their elimination . . . . .
The most devastating of all = = man . . . .

Man who cannot wait for natural balances =
who cannot comprehend the biological
rhythms of life =
but tries = in his own crude way = to
force his will upon all life . .
These forces insects have miraculously conquered =
with methods of meeting hazards as numerous
and ingenious as the hazards themselves . . . . .

Their ability to endure -

their tenacity and adaptability to purpose -

have made them the most

successful of all life upon this earth . . . .

In ponds - - among the grasses of the open fields

- in the high regions of the earth - -

midst all the trees - -

they are as universal as light . . . . .

Zooming and gliding - -

the acme of grace - - -

playing strange rhythms -

flashing tiny lights at twilight -

making use of everything the

environment has to offer . . .

Strong - tough - - tolerant to change -

through millions upon millions of years

attuned to the cosmic order . . .

Upon these tiny lives

the destiny of all life

depends . . . . . .

wareness —

the manifestation of

knowledge and understanding . .

Deep intense knowledge

that reaches the intimate depths

of the living earth . . .

Discovering universal rhythms - -

cognizing that precise order and beauty

underlie all life . . .

Soaring with a bird -
far into the clouds - - -
lightly touching a little flower
in an open field - -
and leaving it there - - - to grow . . . . .
Feeling a passionate kinship with
the integral universe - -
its stars -
wild winds - -
each blade of grass - - -
listening for inaudible songs
of insects in a summer twilight
- - comprehending the myriad fragments
that harmoniously meld to create
its wondrous balance . . . .

In moments of solitude -
awareness enables the mind and spirit
to focus through awe and wisdom
on a world of indisputable loveliness -
- and to evince its eternity . . . .

rowth -

- the force that draws

a towering tree

from a tiny seed -

that has fallen to the earth -

- - that makes each flower

bloom to loveliness - - -

- - - and creates within the human heart

- - - sagaciousness . . . .

ir = water = = energy =

the ineluctable triumvirate . . . . .

The solidity of natural balance

with all its delicacy =

beauty = and flexibility

cannot be transgressed . . . . .

Huge dinosaurs once roamed the lands =

great fern trees flourished = =

until the air = the water and energy

could no longer support them =

and they slowly perished = =

as other lives emerged . . . .

And = even unto this day

as any form of life tends to

over populate its environment

the force of balance =

= the olamic regulator = =

will phase out the excess . . . .

The water of the earth is constant = = =
varying in distribution = never in volume . . .
Energy = = transmutable =
= = = but undiminishable = = =
and the air is forever renewing itself . . . .
A simple equation between
consumption and origin
is the signature of everlasting life . . .
The intricate balance between
the green world =
insects = birds = =
animals and humans
cannot be legislated by man
= = however powerful he may be . . . .
Beyond the human reach
lies the destiny of all = =
resting solely upon
the ineluctable triumvirate
air = water = and energy –
each miraculously perpetuated forever . . . . . .

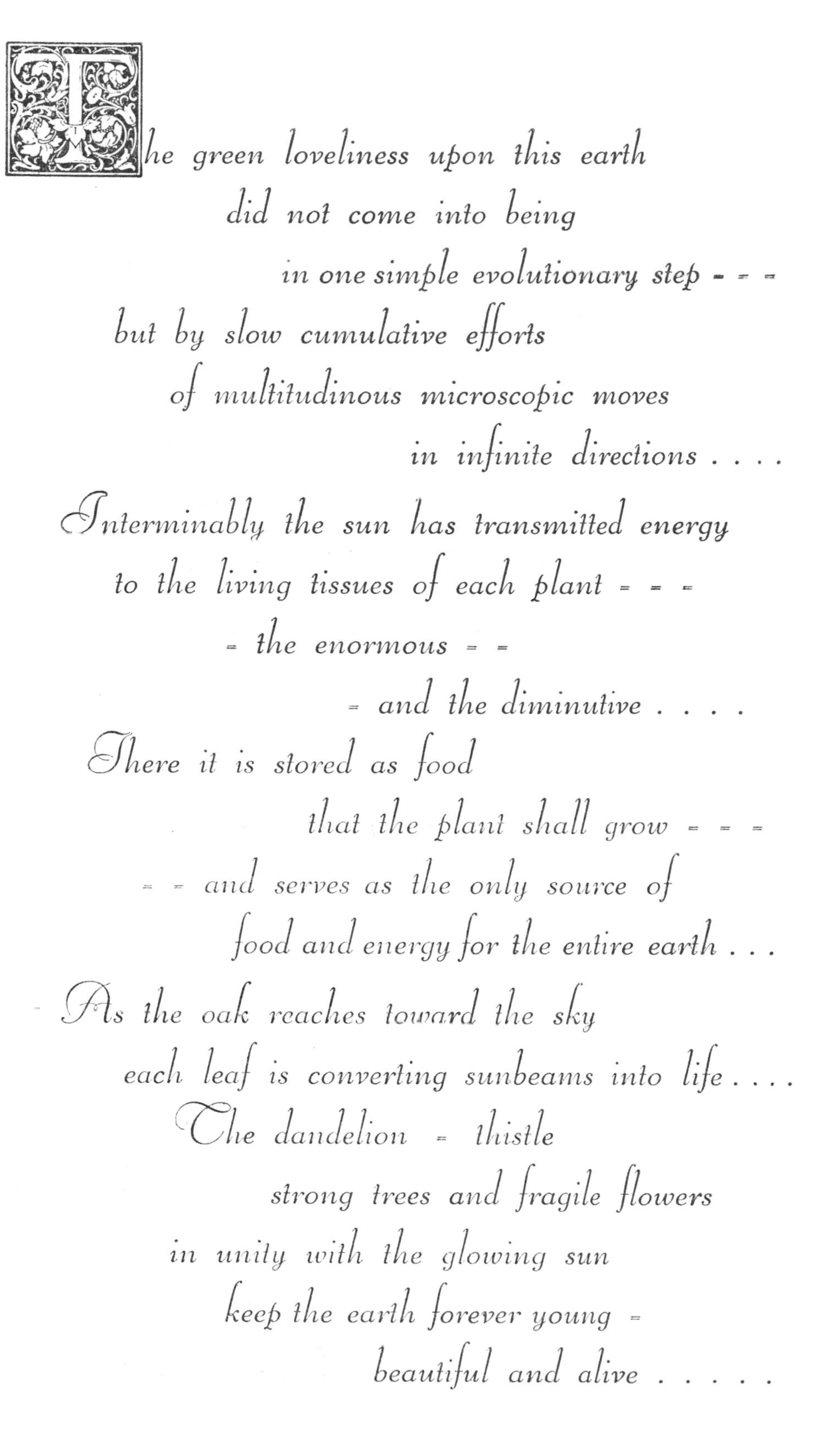

The green loveliness upon this earth
did not come into being
in one simple evolutionary step - - -
but by slow cumulative efforts
of multitudinous microscopic moves
in infinite directions . . . .
Interminably the sun has transmitted energy
to the living tissues of each plant - - -
- the enormous - -
- and the diminutive . . . .
There it is stored as food
that the plant shall grow - - -
- - and serves as the only source of
food and energy for the entire earth . . .
As the oak reaches toward the sky
each leaf is converting sunbeams into life . . . .
The dandelion - thistle
strong trees and fragile flowers
in unity with the glowing sun
keep the earth forever young -
beautiful and alive . . . . .

Seeds –

the most inexpungible force upon this planet - -

- the integral source of perpetual life -

scattered freely by the winds

carried by birds - animals - -

and the waters of streams

and rivers . . . .

Indomitably fertile - - filled with life - -

ready to produce a plant at every

possible opportunity . . .

Unyielding through drought and cold

- through heat and storms

strong -

vigorous -

and resourceful - -

seizing every option to become

a free regenerating life . . .

A seed can hold life within its case many years

until that time when the conditions are right

for its germination - - -

always - - nature knows no haste . . . . . .

Through hereditary genes
each plant perpetuates the pattern
of the one that bore its seed =
yet = each will become a distinct individual . . .
A substance = hormone = lies within
all living cells = = =
directing growth =
regenerating parts = = =
= creating a unique plant
from each tiny seed . . . . . .
Everywhere upon this earth
in the lives of birds = plants = humans - - all - = =
the combination of hereditary genes =
= the substance hormone
= response to surrounding milieu
= and adaptability to change
determines the way each life will grow
to beauty and fulfillment — the commonplace
or fall by the way and perish . . . .
Individualism within heritage =
development while preserving legacy . . . . .

Throughout the high regions of the mountains -
across every valley - -
in oceans and deserts - - -
on solitary islands - - -
plants - self-supporting organisms -
grow to fulfillment -
and all things thrive with them . . . .

When their life span is over
they vanish into the earth and help create
the humus upon which life will flourish
in generations to come . . . .

Aeons after a plant's life is spent -
from the depths of the earth where it has lain -
it releases energy it absorbed from the sun
and becomes a source of radiant heat . . . .

For the beauty of this earth -
- all its food - -
- - for its energy -
the whole world is beholden
to the green plants
blowing in the breeze . . . . .

ime –

the interval between the tides = =

= dawns and twilights

the rotating seasons = = =

and the movement of stars across the skies....

There is a timelessness in nature

as it inevitably moves in harmonious succession

= = = miraculously unhurried......

Flowers bloom again and again

in perfect sequence = =

in ineffable rhythm = birds and fish

are lured back to their place of birth

to carry on the ancient ritual of

perpetuating their kind....

Cosmic time –

totally irreconcilable with

the flurry of minutes and hours

of the clocks of man.....

The human tempo requiring ever increasing

energy creates a cumulative effect

upon the entire cosmos......

An insatiable desire for speed -
with wanton waste and carelessness - -
and lack of understanding - - -
intensifies the drain on available energy - - -

- it takes energy to elicit energy - -
and a millennium of natural development time . . .

Inability to comprehend the dynamics of economies
- - the relationship between environment -
resources and human needs - -
has kept mankind leaping from crises to crises - -
creating desires beyond ability to produce -
demanding power beyond capability to govern -
reaching for achievement without effort - -
heedless of the culminative effect upon all life . . .

Time -
again the contrariety -
human avidity for instantaneousness
against nature's system that waits for
long range developments
or a sequence of fortuitous circumstances . . . .

Endowed with the power of thought -
and the ability to pass cumulated knowledge
from generation to generation - -
mankind is capable of ingenious innovations . . .
Yet - each development has met with
the force of human inertia - -
obstructing amelioration . . . .
Under diligent circumspection - -
continuous euthenics
frees mankind from drudgery - - -
creating time and freedom
to develop an intimacy with nature
that nourishes the mind and spirit - -
- time for reverence -
dreams - - and silence . . . . .
The procession of one form of energy
after another - -
from wood to coal - - to oil and gas - -
wind to steam - electricity to nuclear power
used with proper discretion releases the
power of creativity to all mankind . . . .

Simultaneously with the power
of massive devastation . . .
Diverting colossal amounts of energy
- - resources - - - and human thought
to arsenals of destruction
is depriving all mankind of its
inalienable right to peaceful existence - -
and of manifesting its omnificence
to preserve the legacy of the
environment - - -
- embracing its joy - - and its eternity . . . .
How vast the complexities of the universe !
Each life in subservient union with all - -
alters - and is dependent upon the entirety . . .
Man's knowledge and experience -
with nature's flexibility and diversification
unite with the timelessness of time
to create a world without wanton destruction
- without retaliation - with no need to usurp
- a world of harmony - and loveliness . . . .

Microscopic lives –

tiny fungi - - and mosses - - -

diminutive insects

anemones and corals

of the great oceans - -

massive lives –

huge trees -

animals of the land and seas -

and all the lives between -

humans - frogs - flowers and birds

create the harmonious entirety

each - vital to the intricate balance

upon which the cosmos survives . . .

Man sees innumerable repetitions -

- and wonders why . . . ?

Hears the primeval calls of frogs

in a vernal twilight -

- the diversity of tone - pitches and tempos

that flows into the marshland symphony . . .

Sees millions of insects

swarm over ponds and rivers . . .

Senses multitudinous fragrances
from the living earth -
- its trees and flowers . . .
Encounters olamic similarities - -
- in forms - - colors - - - and purposes
— without a single duplication !
In diversification with imbrication of functions - -
and the potentiality of infinite options -
lie the perpetuity of life . . . .
There is no axiom
to elucidate nature's ultimatum - -
myriads upon myriads of variables
intertwine in diverse ways and times
to create this day and all futurity . . . .
Nothing can be segregated from the entirety - -
individually - each is responsible
for its own being - - alone . .
Yet — it must integrate with the milieu
in which it lives - its sunshine and rains
and all universal life . . . .

Gradualism –

the quintessence of natural change = =

= time for development

and adjustment . . . .

There is an unhurried ebb and flow

of tides = seasons = = days and nights =

ever so slowly rocks become sand =

lakes become marshlands

and the flowers = the insects and birds

slowly adapt to the evolving terrain =

or move on =

leaving a vacuity where other

lives will thrive. . . . .

The signature of nature

is its subtle changes =

and its inexhaustible ingenuity . . . . . .

Flowers host many insects =

insects and birds inhabit various milieus =

and each milieu supports a great diversity of life

exemplifying the wondrous miracle =

= nothing is absolute

= nothing is contradictory

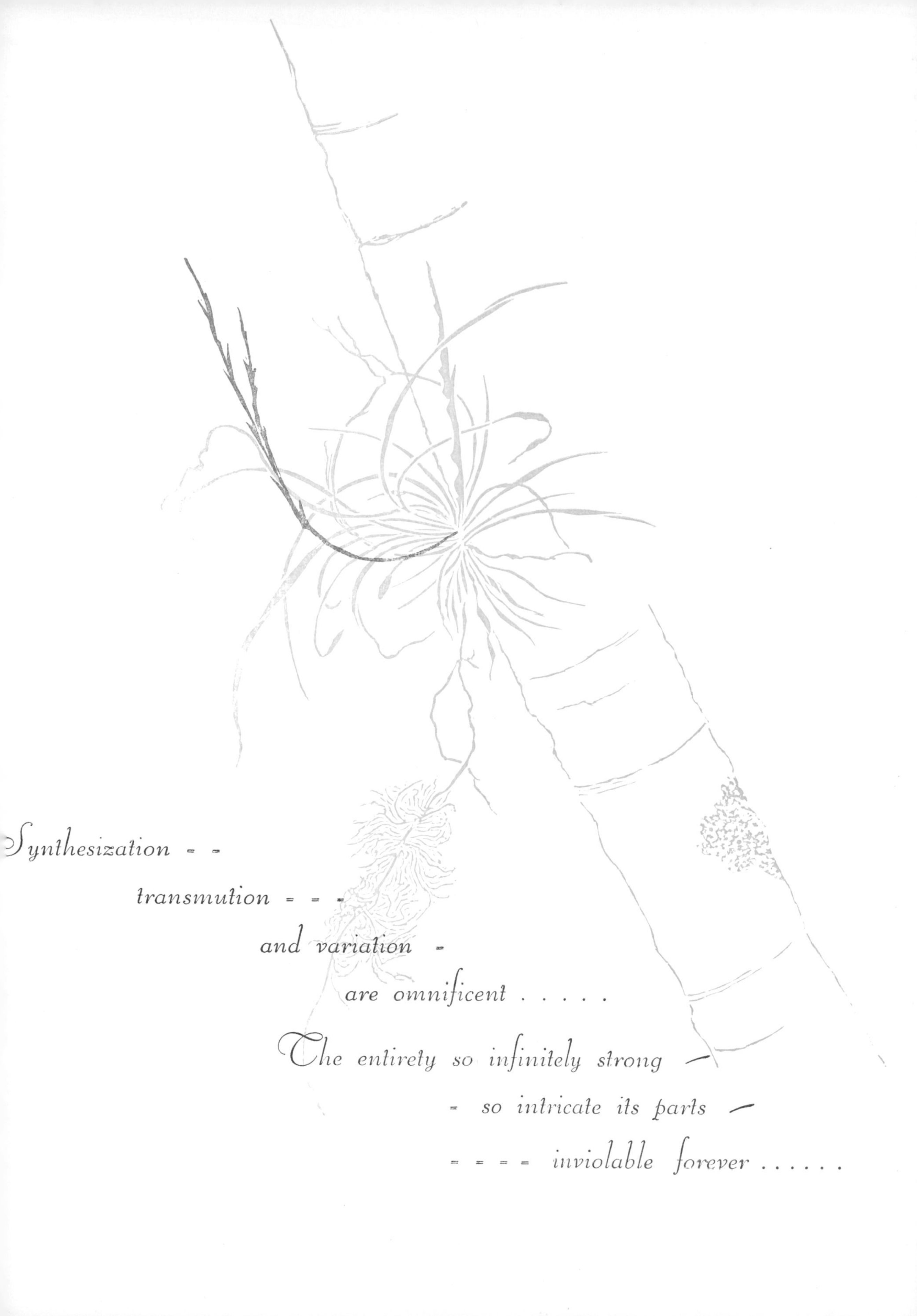
Synthesization - -
transmution - - -
and variation -
are omnificent . . . . .
The entirety so infinitely strong -
- so intricate its parts -
- - - - inviolable forever . . . . . .

If there is ever silence
when not a sound is heard -
if there is ever calm
when the wind has ceased to blow -
if there is ever sunshine
with no clouds or storms above -
if time stands still - - -
and no change evolves - - -

there will be no life on earth . . . . .

For life is action -
life is vicissitude - - - !
To spider - toad - - and reed
to all the trees - and all the birds
the animals and humans
life is striving to become -
in unison with adversities
and auspiciousness . . . .

- - - to this -
mankind adds dreams . . . .

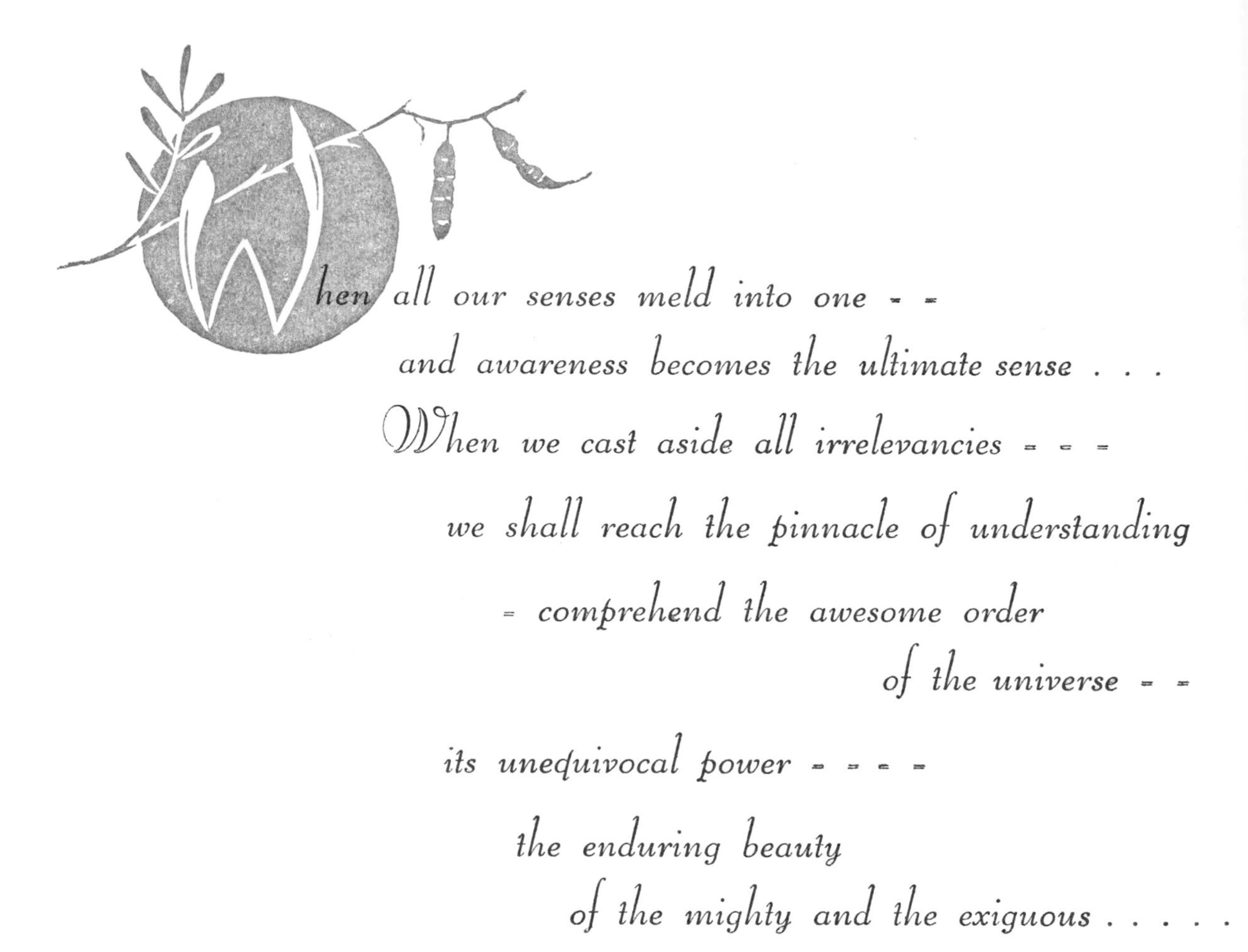

When all our senses meld into one - -
and awareness becomes the ultimate sense . . .
When we cast aside all irrelevancies - - -
we shall reach the pinnacle of understanding
- comprehend the awesome order
of the universe - -
its unequivocal power - - - -
the enduring beauty
of the mighty and the exiguous . . . . .

- - - - then - we shall know . . . . . .

From the waters of the earth
during the primeval span of life's development -
incalculable numbers of fishlike creatures
crawled to the land
initiating multitudinous forms . . . . .

Green plants expanded - -
- insects evolved in steady sequence -
while environmental changes
created life changes - -
all the time - life forms rose - merged - -
became extinct - as individual lives -
while slowly and interminably
life expanded its dimensions -
developing new forms from the old -
and great diversity to synchronize
with ecological requisiteness . . . . .

In this realm of constant change - - -
through the long slow process
of evolutionary inventiveness -
long frayed reptilian scales developed
veins - for strength
- to twist without tearing
flexibility - for flight - -
and fluffiness for insulation -
- - for a life
keyed to lightness - -
with the elimination of every bone
not essential to flight -
a life of the land - the air - - and the waters
a bird . . . .

As lakes = grasslands = forests = mountains =
and deserts became part of the terrene = =
birds with unique traits attuned to each
milieu = evolved . . . . . .

Webbed feet - for those that swim =
narrow wings - for those that soar =
long legs for the waders = =
= beaks with highly specialized shapes
to gather specific foods . . . .

Limitless as the natural habitats =
diversified as the things they feed upon =
resourceful = mobile and beautiful =
— — birds . . . . . .

The runes they sing stir the imagination -
and defy interpretation
- the soft whisperings
- the sudden bursts of radiance
- loud wild cries on the wing
- inexhaustible myriads of notes and melodies
rich and clear - simple and passive -
a tinkling sound in the still air . . . .

To each bird - esoteric expressions -
to the human ear -
an elusive haunting mystery - forever . . . .

Esthetic colors - the manifestation of pure beauty . .
Infinitesimal feather structures -
shifting light and various pigments
create luminosity and vividness . . . .

Radiant reds - blues - yellows and greens
muted shades of browns and grays -
pure whites and pitch blacks
every color - shade - hue and tint
fuse with the most intricate and varied
patterns - making each species unique . . . .

Reflected light =
from the waters = the sky =
and the earth below = =
shadows of leaves and grasses = =
the variance of the seasons =
changing light of each day =
from dawn to the mellowing
light of late afternoon = =
and = the eye of the beholder =
make no color absolute . . . .

In the darkness there is no color . . . .
Fog = mists and rains create many illusions
of size = color and patterns
shrouding each bird in mystery . . . . .

Invariably = the color = patterns
and life style of each bird
are passed from generation to generation =
while the subtleties of evolution occur
within each organism ceaselessly . . . . .

Periodically each bird
renews every feather upon its body =
not at random = = but in methodic order . . .
Some = modify the colors = patterns and
quantity of feathers with the changing seasons.

In regular sequence = as the earth encircles the sun =
birds answer the summons of some cryptic urge = =
= to migrate . . . . !
Those that move the farthest north in springtime
penetrate the extreme south each autumn . . .
Many make non-stop journeys =
covering boundless miles for hours upon hours
= others rest = eat and linger along the way . .
Some fly in large flocks of several kinds =
others in small groups =
= some in the darkness of night = =
silhouetted against the moon
calling and chirping as they go . . . .

An inexplicable arcanum
has intrigued human imagination
through the millenniums . . .
What lures birds from the security
of their nesting grounds
to face unknown hazards . . ?
What triggers the timing of their flight ?
What instinct guides them
through uncharted skies
and always = brings them to
their appointed place on earth
at the appointed hour . . . ?

Flight – a natural phenomenon
the ability to maintain balance
is the essence of harmonious coordination
= each slight motion
performs a definite function
= the shape of every feather
escalates the air flow over the wings
making use of all potential energy . . . .
The least change of air pressure
brings an instant response . . .

Theirs is the power

to fly against the wind

and hold their altitude = =

to fly backward = = forward =

and hover in mid-air . . .

They have the skill to take off

and land with apparent ease = =

to change direction at will = = =

— — and = to soar = = =

to rise in the air on motionless wings

as air currents carry them

far beyond our vision . . . . .

To each = =

its own life = = =

while serving eternity . . . .

The interminable law of the universe . . . . .

They eat nuts

and bury some - perpetuating the growth of trees

search out larvae and grubs that lie

beneath the bark

prolonging the life of the trees . . .

Carriers of seeds - - -

fostering the migration of the plants . . . .

The ultimate regulators

of insect - animal and marine life

and - of bird life itself . . . .

Forever keeping the individual components

in balance

without unwarranted destruction . . .

The futility of man's selection

of any one species -

and condemning it -

is testimony to his ignorance of ecology

- - its rhythms -

- - - and its balances . . . . .

The natural process alone -

in its entirety -

is witness to the interlocking dependencies

that underlie all life . . .

The unceasing succession of life -

the rise - disappearance and merger

of varying forms -

the transmutation - - lives within lives - -

will remain the only living reality . . . . . .

For every life - there is a natural regulator -

vital to the equilibrium of all - -

individuals may be lost -

in the preservation of the universe -

which shall remain forever . .

Deep within your spirit

listen to an enthralling call -

see wings soaring in the boundless sky -

and feel rapture transcending all . . . .

The natural phenomenon
is invincible . . . .

Deserts have enough water to nourish
all the life that populates them . . .
Plants - animals - birds and insects
that inhabit the rain forests
thrive on moisture . . .
The tropics require heat -
and endless sun - -
the arctic regions cold -
with long nights - -
and the temperate zone its seasons . . . .
There is delicacy and completeness
to each milieu
in which life finds the substance
for its every need . . . .

Nature is -
energy - motion - and change
nature is -
beauty - serenity - - and life
everything that is - - and is to be . . .

Nature is —
— — the infinite destiny . . . . . .